ANGLICANISM &
SOUTH INDIA

T0346165

CAMBRIDGE
UNIVERSITY PRESS

University Printing House, Cambridge CB2 8BS, United Kingdom

Published in the United States of America by Cambridge University Press, New York

Cambridge University Press is part of the University of Cambridge.

It furthers the University's mission by disseminating knowledge in the pursuit of education, learning and research at the highest international levels of excellence.

www.cambridge.org
Information on this title: www.cambridge.org/9781107631045

© Cambridge University Press 1943

First published 1943
Re-issued 2014

A catalogue record for this publication is available from the British Library

ISBN 978-1-107-63104-5 Paperback

ANGLICANISM &
SOUTH INDIA

BY

LEONARD HODGSON

Canon of Christ Church and
Regius Professor of Moral and Pastoral Theology
in the University of Oxford

CAMBRIDGE
AT THE UNIVERSITY PRESS
1943

NOTE. *The greater part of this pamphlet was written some five years ago. It had then no direct reference to South India, but set out to consider generally the theological principles involved in the relation of the Anglican communion to non-episcopal churches. In that form it was published in the Spring 1939 number of the American periodical* Christendom. *I have now tried to make clear the relevance of these principles to the issues raised in South India, and offer this revised and enlarged version as a contribution to the present discussions.*

L. H.

Christ Church
  Oxford
April 1943

ANGLICANISM & SOUTH INDIA

I

IT is well known to all the world that the Anglican Church is a church which finds great difficulty in the way of practising intercommunion with more than a very limited number of other Christian bodies. In his sermon at the opening of the 1937 World Conference on Faith and Order at Edinburgh, the [then] Archbishop of York said:

'I speak as a member of one of those churches which still maintain barriers against completeness of union at the Table of the Lord. I believe from my heart that we of that tradition are trustees for an element of truth concerning the nature of the Church which requires that exclusiveness as a consequence, until this element of truth be incorporated with others into a fuller and worthier conception of the Church than any of us hold to-day. But I know that our division at this point is the greatest of all scandals in the face of the world; I know that we can only consent to it or maintain it without the guilt of unfaithfulness to the unity of the Gospel and of God Himself, if it is a source to us of spiritual pain, and if we are striving to the utmost to remove the occasions which now bind us, as we think, to that perpetuation of disunion.'

I have no doubt in my own mind that this Anglican exclusiveness is due to concern in the matter of orders. The Anglican Church is not indifferent to questions of faith, but when the representatives of various churches assembled at the Lausanne Conference in 1927 agreed upon the following statement:

'Notwithstanding the differences in doctrine among us, we are united in a common Christian Faith which is proclaimed in the Holy Scriptures and is witnessed to and

5

safeguarded in the Ecumenical Creed, commonly called the Nicene, and in the Apostles' Creed, which Faith is continuously confirmed in the spiritual experience of the Church of Christ'[1]

this gave what most Anglicans would regard as sufficient agreement in faith to justify intercommunion were there no other obstacles in the way. Elsewhere in Christendom there may be bodies which hold that the acceptance of doctrines defined at a later date than A.D. 381, such, for example, as the doctrine of trans- or consubstantiation, of justification by faith, or of the immaculate conception, is necessary for this purpose, but only a non-representative minority of Anglicans would make any such demand. The situation with which we are confronted is one in which there exist many Christian bodies with which the Anglican Church might be in communion so far as questions of faith are concerned, were it not that the question of orders stands in the way. And the particular question which causes the trouble is that of the apostolic succession.

It is well known that this phrase 'apostolic succession' is patient of many different meanings.[2] The form in which it causes the difficulty is that in which it holds that the minister of the Holy Communion must be one who has been ordained to his office by a bishop who has his place in a succession of episcopal ordinations (or consecrations) going back to apostolic times. It is believed by the Anglican Church that it has a ministry authorised to minister the sacrament by ordination in

[1] From the Report of Section VI. See Bate, *Faith and Order* (London and New York, 1928), p. 466.

[2] See the Report of the Edinburgh Conference, Ch. V (vii) A.

this succession. For its own ministers such authorisation is required by its formularies, and though there may be (and are) Anglicans who set little store by this requirement and have scant respect for the theology involved by it, I have little doubt myself that the Anglican Church as a whole regards itself as committed to this requirement and is not prepared to forsake it or minimise its importance.

It is here that I feel it necessary to avoid raising false hopes by concealing this fact. It is the fashion in some quarters to disregard this fidelity to the doctrine of apostolic succession as though it were the peculiar hobby of a small group described as 'extreme anglo-catholics', whose views can be safely ignored in making plans for the reunion of Christendom. Such an attitude I believe to be profoundly mistaken. Respect for the doctrine of apostolic succession is far more widely diffused among us and deeply ingrained in us than that. It characterises our history, as shown in the lives of such men as Timothy Cutler and Samuel Seabury. I know members of the Church of Ireland who set great store by the fact that when the Vatican decided against the validity of the orders of the Church of England care was taken to say nothing about those of the Church of Ireland, knowing that that church could claim an independent succession unaffected by the accidents which were alleged to invalidate the English claim. The Lambeth Conference may have no legislative authority, or power to bind the church, but its pronouncements are undoubtedly evidence of what is commonly believed and held among us, and both in 1920 and 1930 its resolutions on intercommunion are clearly based upon this doctrine which, moreover, is included in the so-called Chicago-Lambeth Quadrilateral. The actual steps taken by the Church of England in recent years towards the restoration of intercommunion with other bodies have all kept in view the satisfaction of what this doctrine requires; witness the agreements made with the Eastern Orthodox Church, the Old Catholics and the Church of Sweden, and the conditions required in the provisional agreements with the churches of Finland, Latvia and Esthonia.

Among workers for unity there seems to exist in some quarters an optimism which is based upon the assumption that the Anglican Church can easily be persuaded to abandon the doctrine of orders which I have just shown to be implied in the utterances of its responsible leaders and the policy embodied in its official acts. When we try to discover the grounds for this assumption, we find ourselves face to face with a problem the seriousness of which often seems to me to be insufficiently grasped. It is the fundamental problem presented by different conceptions not only of the church, but of the nature of Christianity itself. This difference finds expression both in the fields of history and of theology proper. On one side it is held that recent researches into the history of Christian origins have invalidated whatever historical basis may hitherto have been claimed for the doctrine of apostolic succession. It is also commonly held that theologically the doctrine implies a magical conception of the operation of divine grace which is inconsistent with the principles of true Christianity. From this it is concluded that, since no one in his senses, when once his eyes are opened, will wish to maintain a doctrine which is historically unjustified and theologically superstitious, it cannot be long before it is abandoned by all except that small group of anglo-catholic Anglicans whose eyes are blinded by prejudice. The majority of Anglicans must already be coming to regard it as a *damnosa haereditas*, an encumbrance in their efforts for unity from which they have not yet managed to free themselves and for which they have to apologise.

My own experience of anglicanism from within convinces me that any such estimate of the temper of my fellow-churchmen as a whole is completely mistaken. They do not believe that the holding of this doctrine requires any apology, whether it be considered historically or theologically. The late Canon Streeter, or Dr Newton Flew, may have advanced arguments against its historical foundation convincing to themselves; but there are other scholars, such as C. H. Turner and Canon Broomfield, who read the evidence differently, and among Anglicans the arguments of these other scholars are more widely accepted. Theologically it is denied that the doctrine, rightly understood, is either magical or superstitious—and 'rightly understood' does not mean understood in such a manner as to dissolve away the belief that God wills to give His grace through the appointed means of rightly ordained ministers.

I must emphasise this last point because of its importance for the whole reunion movement. From many of the writings of continental protestants which I have read I have gained the impression that in their eyes fidelity to the principles of the Reformation (which are held to be the principles of true Christianity) requires the rejection of the whole catholic conception of

Christianity, lock, stock, and barrel. Now the Oxford Movement meant for the Anglican Church the recovery of its catholic heritage, and a growing conviction, verified in the experience of the last hundred years, that this antithesis is falsely drawn. I say 'in the experience' because it is clear that the intellectual problems involved have by no means yet been solved. We have proved that it is possible to live and worship together as sons both of the Reformation and of the historic catholic church. But this is regarded by many of our continental fellow-Christians as merely another instance of English in-difference to logic, and we must confess that we have not yet solved the intellectual problems provided by the coexistence of protestantism and catholicism in one church. If we had, we should be able to show our continental brethren how the breach could be healed to their satisfaction as well as to ours. As it is, they suspect that we are only able to maintain our own *façade* of unity either through sheer intellectual laziness or because neither our protestantism nor our catholicism is the genuine article.

But we are realists. When we contemplate Christendom, we find it impossible to believe that either catholicism or protestantism taken alone expresses the full truth of Christianity. We find it impossible to believe that the unity of Christendom will be achieved through either, so to speak, 'swallowing' the other. We therefore conclude that the alternative to the reconciliation of the two in one church is an arrangement in which, when Christians are sorted out of their present muddle and have crystallised around one or other of these two poles, the two camps will continue until the day of judgment separated by a gulf which only men as individuals can cross, crossing it as converts or perverts according to the point of view. This seems to us an unsatisfactory picture to contemplate as the goal of the reunion movement, and so we cherish the hope that our apparently illogical makeshift of a church may turn out to provide more valuable food for thought than appears on the surface.

But if this be our hope, then it is clear that we shall not be likely to respond to any appeals to take steps towards unity which involve abandoning either our protestant or our catholic pretensions. We do not regard the Oxford Movement as a regrettable relapse into a discredited catholicism. We regard it as the recovery of a catholic heritage which is of value to ourselves at present, and which we hold in trust to share with the rest of Christendom if and when our fellow-Christians come to perceive its value and to desire it for themselves. In this connection I may here repeat some words I wrote more than ten years ago, which still seem to me to express a typically Anglican outlook.

'For the Anglican, unity means unity vertically down the ages as well as horizontally across the face of the earth, unity with that little company in the Upper Room at Jerusalem as well as with fellow-Christians now alive in America, India and Japan. When an Anglican sets out to baptise a convert, he sets out to baptise him into that fellowship; when the Anglican priest stands before the altar to celebrate the Holy Communion, or a lay-reader holds a mission service for half a dozen souls in some isolated region of Montana or Wyoming, that which is being done is an official act of the whole society functioning in that place. The members of a little gathering of twentieth-century Christians in an out-of-the-way corner of the world are to be assured that they are worshipping in communion with Peter and Andrew, James and John, the rest of that company, and the whole company of "just men made perfect" from that day to this.

'This being his aim, the Anglican asks how that unity can be secured. He notices that in any earthly society unity and continuity from generation to generation seem to depend on two factors interwoven like two strands of a single rope: the outward continuity of organisation and the inward continuity of spirit, faith and practice. He notices, for example, that if a body of trustees are challenged as to their right to continue administering some endowment, they have to make good their position by showing both that they have been appointed constitutionally in accordance with the accepted custom of the trust, and that in their administration they are carrying out the intentions of the founder as he would like them to be carried out were he alive at the time. He concludes that he cannot rightly exercise less care in matters spiritual than is required in matters temporal, that he cannot offer to baptise into the fellowship of the Apostles if he is careless about either strand of the rope which links the Church of to-day to the Church of the Upper Room.'[1]

The action taken by the Church of England in its negotiations with the churches of Finland, Latvia and Esthonia illustrates this attitude, and shows, moreover, that on the side of outward organisation the apostolic succession is regarded as one of those valuable elements in the catholic tradition which we treasure for ourselves and wish to share with others. It therefore seems clear that the Anglican Church is not at all likely to respond favourably to any suggestions which would require it to treat its apostolic succession as a thing of little value. Any hopes of a united Christendom which is to include Anglicanism must include the hope that the rest of

[1] From *Essays in Christian Philosophy* (London and New York, 1930), p. 144.

Christendom will welcome the opportunity of sharing in this treasure which has been given to the Anglican Church to be its contribution to the riches of the whole united body.

But see what this means. Our hope must include the hope that a way will have been found to reconcile this belief that the apostolic succession is a treasure with the belief that to regard it as such is apostasy from true Christianity! To refuse to face this fact is to behave like the proverbial ostrich. The reunion movement as a whole, in its world-wide aspect, will not have faced realities until it has opened its eyes to contemplate steadily the problem of reconciling the sons of the Reformation with the heirs of Trent. And it is no good treating the problem of the Anglican position about orders as anything less than a subdivision of this problem, or thinking that it can be disposed of by itself without raising these wider and deeper issues.

If this be so, it is idle to look for any speedy solution of the problem. The issues involved are so deep and far-reaching that to solve their difficulties will require a resolute and determined intellectual effort. At present it has hardly been begun, and we cannot expect to bring it to a successful conclusion unless we are prepared to persevere in it for no short period of time.

Are we then led to the pessimistic conclusion that for this indefinitely lengthy period the Anglican Church must continue to acquiesce in 'the greatest of all scandals in the face of the world' by maintaining the present barriers against union at the Table of the Lord? And must it reject all proposals for union with other churches which do not provide for the immediate extension of episcopal ordination to all the ministers of the Holy Communion in the united body? These are the questions which have now to be faced.

II

For anyone who has had borne in upon him the reality of the present situation—not merely the scandal in the face of the world, but also the inner wounding of the Body of Christ—it is impossible to rest content with things as they are. But when an Anglican advocates the raising of the existing barriers to intercommunion, or the approval of such a scheme as that of the proposals for union in South India, he is inevitably met by the argument that he is allowing his heart to run away with his head. The maintenance of the barriers, it is urged, is demanded by theological principle, and to think that unity in accordance with the will of God can be built upon neglect of or indifference to theological principle is sentimentality at its worst. Theological principle forbids us to equate episcopal and non-episcopal ministries; theological principle requires us to observe 'the general rule of the Anglican Churches that members of the Anglican Churches should receive the Holy Communion only from ministers of their own Church'; at Lambeth in 1930 the Anglican bishops came dangerously near to compromising with theological principle, as indeed they recognised when they appended to their recommendations the words 'we would point out that the very special circumstances and the very strict regulations specified in this Regulation of themselves show that we are not departing from the rule of our Church that the minister of the Holy Communion should be a priest episcopally ordained'.[1]

It is clear, then, that if any proposal for a relaxation of the present restrictions is to have any chance of acceptance it must be based on grounds of theological principle.

Let us first try to state more precisely what the present situation is. The Lambeth Conference may have no binding authority, but in actual practice few Anglican bishops or clergy feel justified in disregarding its resolutions. Those resolutions, while referring to the 'rule' that the minister of the Holy Communion should be a priest episcopally ordained, allow a diocesan bishop to authorise the admission of baptised communicants of other Christian bodies to communion at an Anglican service in certain circumstances, and it is the custom to include in these circumstances conferences of Christians gathered together from various denominations for the purpose of setting forward the cause of unity. But permission to Anglicans to communicate at non-episcopal services is restricted to 'special areas where the ministrations of an Anglican Church are not available for long periods of time or without travelling great distances'. The result is that at conferences for the promotion of unity Anglican clergy feel themselves able with a clear conscience to invite to an Anglican service baptised communicant members of other bodies who may be present, but cannot approve of the Anglicans present communicating at a non-

[1] Report of the Lambeth Conference, 1930, Resolution 42. Cp. Resolution 12 (B) of 1920.

15

episcopal service.[1] This barrier to 'reciprocity' pains the heart and makes it ask the head whether theological principle does indeed demand its retention.

Now however firmly an Anglican may believe it to be the will of God for His Church that the sacrament of Holy Communion should only be celebrated by priests episcopally ordained, and however strong may be his conviction that in the apostolic succession the Anglican Church has entrusted to it a treasure to be faithfully guarded for the ultimate benefit of all Christendom, he cannot regard this inestimable blessing as a thing to boast about or as having been conferred upon his church in recognition of its superior merit. His Christianity and his common sense combine to make this impossible. His Christianity teaches him that boasting is excluded, and forbids either individual or church to claim that the gracious gifts of God are given in reward for human merit. What common sense has to say about the matter demands a paragraph to itself.

On an objective and impartial reading of the history of the sixteenth and succeeding centuries it is surely impossible to maintain that either those churches which have maintained or those which have lost the apostolic succession have done so with a full conscious realisation of all that was involved, or with full control over the course of their own history. There are some churches, such as the Church of Finland, which have lost it through sheer accident. There are other churches, notably

[1] Thus it often happens that when such a gathering is held on the continent of Europe, the only way in which those present can communicate together is if the celebrant is a visiting Anglican priest and not a minister of the church of the country whose hospitality they are enjoying.

among the Lutherans, in which it was not lost through any desire or deliberate intention to repudiate it, but because when they were forced to choose between the retention of the episcopate and fidelity to what they believed to be true doctrine, they chose the giving up of the former as the lesser evil. What in this respect was true of certain Lutheran churches in the sixteenth century was equally true of Methodism in the eighteenth. And even in the case of churches of the Reformed tradition, and of Independency, it is impossible to maintain that what they repudiated was the episcopal apostolic succession as such. The form in which they were acquainted with it was one which in their eyes had become the source of so much corruption that it seemed necessary to make a new beginning, and the effort to restore the primitive purity of the church led in the one case to the establishment of a succession through the presbyterate and in the other through the calling by the congregation. When one reflects upon the history of the sixteenth century, and all the tangled skein of motives, political, ecclesiastical, doctrinal, moral and religious through which the Western Church became divided, it is impossible to apportion praise or blame to this or that body for having retained or let slip this or that element in the common heritage of the past. We may be thankful that out of the storm and stress of that age our Anglican ancestors emerged with their episcopal succession unimpaired. But if England had 'gone' Presbyterian like Scotland, how many of us who as born Anglicans are staunch Episcopalians would not have been equally staunch Presbyterians? We may with grateful hearts acknowledge that we are episcopalian by the grace of

God, but if we are honest we must acknowledge also that we are episcopalian by the accident of history; and this must surely affect our attitude towards those whose zeal for righteousness and honest desire to find and do God's will led them in those difficult days along other paths.

There can be no theological principle more fundamental than the character of God as made known to us in the biblical revelation. This revelation is given in its fullness in Christ, the incarnate Word. When we look back over the Old Testament with the revelation in Christ as our guide to its interpretation, we see that the whole Bible bids us think of God as demanding of man the honest pursuit of what he believes to be right.[1] We are not to think of Him as one who would punish us for accidentally spilling the salt, or sitting down thirteen at a table, or going to sea on a Friday. But if this be so, we cannot think of God as penalising either men or churches for failing to secure such a thing as the apostolic succession, if what they were doing was honestly seeking to find and do His will as it appeared to them in the circumstances of their time.

This is what we should be doing if we were to refuse to regard the sacraments of non-episcopal bodies as in every way equal to our own on the ground that they are not celebrated by ministers episcopally ordained. For every ministry and every sacrament is what God makes them, and to regard any ministry or sacrament as deficient is to believe that God withholds from it the fullness of the gift which it is intended to convey. When

[1] I have argued this more fully in my book *The Grace of God in Faith and Philosophy* (Longmans, 1936), pp. 86 ff. See also *Towards a Christian Philosophy* (Nisbet, 1943), pp. 139 ff.

we think of those churches with which we Anglicans are sufficiently one in faith to invite their members to communicate at our altars, and to believe that we might be united were it not for our differences on the subject of orders, we may not allow ourselves to have any doubts about the blessings, sacramental and otherwise, which God gives them equally with ourselves. As we thank God for our own history which has preserved for us the apostolic succession which we long to share with them, we realise that to think or speak depreciatively about their sacraments is a blasphemous contradiction of the most fundamental theological principle known to us.

We would seem, then, to be in a dilemma, drawn in one direction by the theological principle which requires us to regard episcopal ordination as willed by God for the ministers of His sacraments, and in another by the theological principle which requires us to recognise the equality of episcopalian and non-episcopalian sacraments. What are we to do?

I would suggest that we can be faithful to both principles if we distinguish between God's will for His Church in its unity and His will for it in its present divided condition. There is no inconsistency in maintaining both that we hold the apostolic succession in trust to be our contribution to the fulfilment of God's will in the united church of the future, and also that in this interim period of disorganisation between the disruption of the past and the reunion of the future, He wills us to recognise the equality of His sacramental activity in episcopal and non-episcopal bodies alike.

Do I then advocate an immediate abolition of all restrictions and barriers to intercommunion? I do not.

There is a group of considerations arising out of another approach to the subject which have not yet been mentioned but must now be taken into account. For many Anglicans it is not only the question of the ministry which stands in the way of intercommunion; there is also the conviction that the sacrament of Holy Communion is a corporate activity of the church expressing its fellowship. Intercommunion between the members of divided churches is a self-contradiction, and a pretence of non-existent unity. When a group of Christians drawn from different churches hold a joint communion service, they either arrogate to the group the right to function as a church, or else they combine a number of acts of individualistic lawlessness into the acting of a lie.

Here there are two strains of thought which need to be disentangled. There is the objection to intercommunion on the ground that it dishonestly conceals the divided state of the church, and there is the objection to members of an *ad hoc* group participating as individuals in an action which can only have any meaning if it is the action of a church. These must be considered separately.

The objection that intercommunion conceals the divided state of the church presents a real difficulty and must be taken seriously. There is indeed force in the contention that we should not hide our disunity from ourselves by behaving as though it were not so. So long as we are not one united fellowship, we have no right to ignore this tragic fact at the altar. So long as we apathetically tolerate this state of affairs, we ought to be made to feel the pain of it. Here again I find myself still in agreement with what I wrote in 1930:

'*Intercommunion is unity*;[1] and the steps towards it are the findings of ways to such agreements on faith and order as make it possible for all without qualm of conscience. To initiate immediate intercommunion as though these preliminary steps were unnecessary is like allowing a deep wound to heal over on the surface when its cure requires it to fill up with healthy tissue from within outwards. The question when the skin may be allowed to grow over the wound is an empirical question to be decided by the doctor in charge of the case, and the nurse who works under him must wait for his word before this step is taken. In the life of the Church the local minister is the nurse, and it is not for him to decide whether the relations between his communion and another are such as to justify intercommunion with them. It may be hard and painful for him to refrain from taking this step, but that is as it should be. Disunity should be painful; but the pain should be welcomed as a spur to drive us on towards its healing, not succumbed to as a temptation to conceal it.'[2]

This comparison of the local minister with the nurse who must act under authority leads on to our second point, the objection to the individualism involved in an *ad hoc* group of Christians arranging for a service which is not corporately authorised by their respective churches. This difficulty also needs to be taken seriously.

Let us again review the existing situation. The bishops of the Anglican communion have agreed that they will not call in question the action of any one of their number who in his own sphere of jurisdiction sanctions under certain circumstances the invitation of baptised communicant members of other churches to communicate at Anglican altars. Although it is argued by some that this decision of the bishops has no authority, and that

[1] I.e. as distinguished from reciprocal open communion.
[2] From *Essays in Christian Philosophy*, p. 159.

a bishop who acts in accordance with it is himself committing an act of individualistic lawlessness,[1] this view is not, so far as I can judge, generally accepted by Anglicans. Many, if not most, of us would feel that if what we do is done with the approval of our local bishop and in accordance with a resolution of the episcopate as a whole, it is not an individualistic act of our own, but an authoritatively recognised act of the church to which we belong. For this reason we do not believe that we should be justified in going beyond the limits for which permission can be given under the Lambeth resolutions.

So far as the circumstances are concerned, the maintenance of those limits seems to me for the present to be right. They allow an Anglican 'open' communion service in two cases: (a) where there are Christians within reach of Anglican ministration but out of reach of their own, and (b) where there is a gathering of Christians assembled for the purpose of setting forward the cause of unity. The underlying principle is clearly this. Where churches are continuing to live side by side as separated bodies, this fact should be recognised, and the members of each communicate in the fellowship to which they belong. But where this is impossible, or where there is an assembly for the purpose of working to end the divisions and restore a united fellowship, the 'general rule' can be waived without involving the danger of premature intercommunion concealing the divisions and delaying their cure.

The conclusion to which we are brought by the appeal

[1] E.g. by Dr W. H. Dunphy in *Oecumenica*, Vol. IV, No. 4, p.684 (London, S.P.C.K. January 1938).

to theological principle is that the Church of England would be right to sanction *reciprocal* open communion services in those circumstances in which Anglican open communion services are already sanctioned. In 1930 the bishops took a step towards this in circumstance (*a*), though with considerable hesitation and apparently some misgiving lest their Christian charity should be leading them into disregard of theological principle. They took no step forward in respect of circumstance (*b*). We can now see that these hesitations and misgivings may be removed, and that theological principle not only confirms the action taken, but demands its extension to circumstance (*b*). Such action could be taken by the authorities of the Church of England without compromising the principles for which Anglicanism stands. It would enable us not as individuals but as loyal representatives of our church to recognise in practice, in deed as well as in word, the equality of the ministries and sacraments of our fellow-Christians from whom for the time being we are divided. It would do more than anything else to convince Christendom as a whole that the Anglican Church is serious in its often expressed desire for unity.

III

Any consideration of the attitude to be taken by loyal members of the Church of England towards the South India proposals must be prefaced by a *caveat*. We are not asking whether the Church of England, or the bishops of the Anglican communion, should sanction or forbid the proposed union. Any such attempt to interfere with the autonomy of the Church of India, Burma and

Ceylon would be intolerable. We are not in a position to appreciate the circumstances in which its four southern dioceses have to do their work, or to judge whether in those circumstances retention of full membership in the Anglican communion may not be too high a price to pay for continued disunity. Our task is simply to try to answer the academic question whether participation in the proposed union would involve disloyalty to Anglican theological principles.

Those principles, as we have examined them, give rise to three propositions:

1. We believe it to be the will of God for His Church that its sacraments should be administered by a ministry ordained through the apostolic succession of bishops. We believe that we are one of the churches of Christendom who hold such a ministry in trust for the united church of the future.

2. We cannot refuse to recognise the equality of the ministries and sacraments of other churches on the ground that in the historical disruptions they lost the succession.

3. We must therefore distinguish between the action required by the will of God in a united and a disunited Christendom.

The South India scheme, as I understand it, conforms to the first of these propositions in that it provides for the extension to the whole united church of a sacramental ministry ordained in the episcopal succession. It is thus a step towards the fulfilment of the vocation of Anglicanism to share with the whole of Christendom the privilege with which it has been entrusted during the years of division. But during the negotiations which have now been carried on for upwards of twenty years, it has become clear that this is an aim which cannot be achieved in full completeness all at once. Nor does it seem likely that any further prolongations of the already lengthy discussions would bring this result nearer. In this respect those who now wish to go forward to the consummation of the union cannot justly be accused of wishing to act with undue haste.

We have therefore to ask whether the delay of a generation in the full achievement of this aim, and the existence during this period of irregularities which will disappear with the passage of time, need oblige loyal Anglicans to refuse this opportunity of fulfilling in part the specifically Anglican vocation in Christendom. Here our second and third propositions of fundamental principle surely give clear guidance. If we are bound to acknowledge the equality of non-episcopal with episcopal ministries and sacraments in divided churches during the period of disruption, we cannot rate lower those same ministries and sacraments during the formative period of the proposed Church of South India. And if, as we have seen, we can approve of reciprocal open communion on occasions when representatives of divided churches are gathered together with the common aim of seeking to heal their divisions, *a fortiori* we must approve of it in the life of a church which is passing through this formative period for the express purpose of achieving this aim.

There was a time when I thought that the principle that Christians must not act in their divided state as though they were all united was a principle which forbade all intercommunion between members of divided churches, and especially between those with episcopal and non-episcopal ministries. I now see that the conclusion to be drawn from this premise is precisely the opposite. It is that we must be prepared to tolerate irregularities during the period of disruption which would be unjustifiable in a united Christendom. We have therefore to consider on its merits, as it comes before us, each proposal for recognition of ministries or for common participation in the sacrament of Holy Communion. Having given such consideration as I am able to the proposals contained in the South India Scheme, I have come to the conclusion that they merit the whole-hearted approval of loyal Anglicans who wish to see their church fulfil the obligations and rise to the responsibilities of its catholic heritage. It is for the Indians to decide. If they decide to go ahead, I hope the Church of England will cheer them on.